Ashley "Empowers" Brown

Dating with Purpose

A STORY OF HOW GOD TURNED A HOT MESS INTO A HOUSEWIFE

D0968091

Contents

Dedication

To my husband Carrington Brown:

Carrington, you are my answered prayer. You were everything I asked for, plus so many bonuses! I'm still waiting for you to admit that you are really an angel, but I know you can't blow your cover!

To Heather Lindsey:

Heather, you are such a light in this world! Thank you for walking in your calling and being a positive example in my life and the lives of countless others. You are a beacon of hope and you have impacted my life in such a positive way!

Introduction

God is the great author of romance—I am not. I am inspired to write my love story because it still amazes me that I have one to share. I can't tell you how many times I hoped, wished, and prayed for the wrong relationships to result in marriage. Looking back, I am grateful that God overrode my desires time and time again. When I was 23, I made a decision to do things differently. I stopped entertaining men who didn't share my vision when it came to faith and relationships and I started preparing to be a wife…with no prospects in sight. Being a wife, is not a presence of a ring, it's the presence of your character. I knew that in order to be "found" (Proverbs 18:22), I needed to stop functioning in the spirit of a girlfriend and develop a wife mindset. I decided to believe #ByFaith that my desire to be married wasn't just a pipe dream, but a whisper from God that His best was coming. For years, I have read about couples' testimonies, not quite sure how mine would play out, and now, I have my own testimony to share.

Many people ask me what it means to "Date with Purpose." Simply put, it's pursuing healthy relationships with God at the center. My story is not your traditional Christian courtship story, and in many ways, I am thankful for that, because I have been able to witness how in God's garden of grace, even a broken tree can bear fruit. My hope is that my story inspires you to drop the pen that is scribbling over your love story so that God can pick it up to illustrate His perfect plan for your life. Considering my marriage one of my biggest accomplishments, I am happy to share with you how God turned this hot mess into a housewife.

CHAPTER 1
My Story

Growing up, I witnessed many dysfunctional relationships ; when I was old enough to date, I experienced my fair share of them as well. I never truly knew how to date, or what standards I should have and I was discouraged by all the failed relationships I saw around me. I did not grow up in church and I can't recall seeing any couples who were happily married. My parents divorced when I was very young and I have very few memories of being in a two-parent household, although it was something I always fantasized about. As I got older I witnessed a close family member go through custody battles and mistreatment due to the repeated cycle of dysfunction in her relationships. I remember going to court with her when I was in high school. As I sat in the back of the courtroom waiting for her hearing, I listened to case after case of broken families appear before a hurried judge trying to negotiate personal family matters. I couldn't believe it. At first, I was fearful. I thought, "Could this be my life one day? Do all marriages result in divorce?" Something deep down inside reminded me that in life I didn't have to make every mistake myself, but I could learn from the mistakes of others. I allowed that courtroom to be my first lesson. Silently, I took mental notes of all the things I didn't want to repeat.

I'm from a small suburb near Wichita, Kansas. I was raised around middle-class families although we were not. My mother was fortunate enough to receive a housing voucher so we could live in a nice area, rather than the projects where most families on governmental assistance lived. She was a single mother for the majority of my life, raising four girls on her own. My father was deported back to Nigeria after being incarcerated for almost 5 years. He eventually remarried and had my brothers and sister and built a lucrative empire in a few short years. Although I didn't have the most glamorous upbringing, I was happy. I had moments of missing my dad, wishing that he could accompany me to father-daughter dances or pick me up from school, but even as a little girl, I was mature enough to accept my childhood for what it was. The absence of my father had a profound impact on the trajectory of my life and I give him credit for allowing me to learn independence and teaching me responsibility in an unconventional way. God has used my father to bless me tremendously, and I will forever be grateful for that. I truly believe that growing up in a neighborhood where most of the families were comprised of both a mom and dad, and were financially stable, inspired me to have that for myself one day.

Being raised by a single mother, we struggled financially. I was often frustrated that I couldn't participate in dance lessons or attend certain events because my mom didn't have the time to run us around or the money to pay for it. Some might say I had the best of both worlds because I had one parent who struggled to make ends meet and another who was a multi-millionaire.

This has never been something I boasted about because my reality for the majority of my life was poverty. At the age of 14, I finally thought I could "do something about it," so I got a job. Yes, a job. I started working at the Dollar Tree down the street from my house. I said that I was 16 years old on the job application in order to meet the age requirement. I learned how to manage my money and be resourceful. I would get dressed up and go to work, all while finding my own transportation since I was too young to drive. I would either get there by asking my older sister to drive me, or by my good ol' K'swiss (walking shoes).

Not only did I start working at a young age, but I also started clubbing at a young age. I grew up in a predominantly Caucasian neighborhood and when my mom got married and divorced for the second time, we ended up moving to a neighborhood that was culturally diverse. By the time I was 16, I had already been to the club, smoked for the first time, and tasted my first sip of alcohol. At my new high school, I was inspired to start making better choices because I finally felt like I fit in. After having classes with a few girls on the cheerleading squad, I was inspired to get involved at school. The cheerleaders were smart, fit, and ambitious and encouraged me to try out for the team, unlike my other school where you had to practically be in gymnastics your entire life before even considering trying out. I felt confident that I could make the squad (with no experience). It was one of the best decisions I made because it not only changed my environment, I ended up getting a scholarship to cheer in college.

CHAPTER 2

A Hot Mess in My Sunday's Best

My unhealthy dating patterns began in college, where I was able to fully express my inner hot mess. I was a cheerleader, a business major, at the top of my class, a national pageant competitor, in a sorority, and I had a list of dreams and goals that I was ferociously checking off my list. I felt worthy because of all my accomplishments, but I was lacking genuine purpose. Although it looked like I "had it all together" on the outside, I was spiritually immature. I believed in God, but I didn't have a real relationship with Him. I went to God when I needed to pass a class, keep a toxic boyfriend, or to ensure that I wasn't pregnant. I had ridiculous requests, and I never took the time to consult Him on His will for my life.

When I was single, I didn't know how to be single. My worth was completely wrapped up in having a man or getting a man. It always felt as if I was wastefully trying to fill a void that grew deeper and deeper after every failed relationship. No one ever educated me on the importance of purity or purposefully dating. I started dating based on the relationships I saw around me. This meant having friends with benefits, being intimate before marriage, and putting my boyfriends before God. It didn't take me long to see that this pattern of dating wasn't getting me anywhere. Many of my friends were having kids out of wedlock, suffering from habitual breakups, taking frequent trips to STD clinics, and infidelity appeared to be the norm. Deep down, I knew I wanted something different; looking back, I see how the Holy Spirit was always with me, offering me wisdom despite my stubbornness and constant neglect.

A week before I graduated from college in December 2010, I was sitting in my room at my sorority house. It was then that I had an encounter with the Holy Spirit. At that point in my life, I was smoking multiple times a week, dating without any intention of being in a relationship, and still emotionally connected to men from my past relationships. That night, the Holy Spirit revealed to me that in order to have all that God had for me, I needed to change my ways. This meant that I needed to stop drinking, smoking, and having pre-marital sex. I realized that the type of husband I desired would not be attracted to the girl I was then—a hot mess. This revelation hit me like a ton of bricks. In that moment, I wanted to do better. I wanted God to help me become the woman He intended me to be. This was all the confirmation I needed to begin to change. I felt hopeful and excited to see what He had in store for me. I knew it was not a coincidence that He chose that time and place to speak to me. I was a week away from graduating from college and I had my whole life ahead of me. That encounter led me into my journey of truly living for God and building a relationship with Him. I say *journey* because my life didn't change instantly. I *still battled* sin, and my mind needed intensive renewal. I lost friends, I gained friends, and I didn't quite know how to deal with that. My lifestyle began to change and I was still trying to deal with the unfamiliarity of this new person I was becoming.

After I graduated from college, I moved to Washington, D.C to work on Capitol Hill. During this time, I really knew I was changing, but I did not know how to adjust. I would get invitations to go to the club or to attend happy hours, but as I was growing spiritually, I slowly began to lose interest in the clubbing scene. Getting dressed up and going out with my friends used to be the norm, but it didn't seem to fit my lifestyle anymore. I would spend the evening sorting through my closet trying to find a cute outfit, all to come home tipsy and upset with myself for wasting my time. I would dance and watch my friends having fun talking to random guys, but I didn't enjoy it anymore. Free drinks and IHOP after the club only captured my interest for so long. I tried to convince myself that I still fit in, that I was still "about that life," but the club scene wasn't making me happy. I would ask myself, "am I the only one who is fed up with doing the same thing every single weekend?" No matter how hard I tried, I knew I had to stop resisting the transformation that was so evidently taking place within me. My desires had changed and no one around me could relate to the shift occurring in my spiritual life. I felt like the experience I had that night in the sorority house spoiled the party-girl lifestyle for me. My world was the same, but I knew deep down I wasn't. I had to get over the fear of being alone and missing out on all the "fun" in order to align myself with my destiny.

CHAPTER 3
Wounds to Wisdom

Ironically, the same night I got the "get your life together" memo in the sorority house, I met my next ex-boyfriend. I have always desired serendipitous moments, so I thought that since we met the same day I had the encounter with the Holy Spirit, it was a "sign." That night, I logged onto Facebook and noticed someone sent me his information. We were chatting, talking about God, and I was so excited to meet someone who was Christian and had a desire to wait until marriage. After a few short months of getting to know one another, we became boyfriend and girlfriend. At the time, I was finishing up my fellowship program in Washington, DC and I had a choice to either move back to boring Kansas with my mom, or to move to big-city Houston to pursue a relationship that could potentially lead to marriage. "Hmmm, let me see…" I thought to myself. "Boring Kansas, or big-city Houston?" I chose Houston. The next thing I knew, I was contacting my relatives in Houston to set up temporary living arrangements until I found a job and a place to live.

After nine short months of living in Houston, it was obvious that this relationship still didn't resemble the kind of relationship God wanted me to be in. The "waiting until marriage" ended up being a fluke; I should have known because, early on, I saw signs that he wasn't as disciplined as he claimed to be. The first time we hung out, he was all over me. I was caught off-guard because he was the one who constantly publicized the fact that he rededicated his life to Christ, and that he was abstaining until marriage. His actions didn't line up with his words. The relationship went from good, to bad, to ugly very quickly. At the end of the day, we were both very immature. We went through each other's phones, had temporary breakups that wouldn't even last 24 hours, and more. We desired to have a relationship that was healthy, but we weren't emotionally ready. We argued more than need-be, and neither my family nor my friends were a fan of him. After sin and lust contaminated yet another relationship, God had my attention. When it came to relationships, I didn't have the blueprint on what steps to take to have a successful relationship;

it was trial-and-error. I thought that, since I met someone who talked about God and went to church, it was a divine assignment. Hindsight is 20/20, but while I was in the relationship, I didn't realize that my relationship with God was on the verge of failure.

November 11, 2011 was the date that God gave me to permanently break up with my Houston boyfriend. Originally, I was open to the idea, because our relationship was not going well, but at the same time, I had *just* moved to Houston, and believed our relationship still had potential despite our disobedience. Regardless of my optimism, I had many hunches that I was supposed to break up with him. As the date got closer, I noticed our relationship taking a turn for the worse. We became willing to negotiate on what we considered "taking it too far."

Our hearts were misaligned and we lacked the discipline to set sexual boundaries. My convictions grew stronger about remaining in yet another unhealthy relationship, and I started to look forward to the freedom of being single again.

When November 11th came around, I remember avoiding the thought of us breaking up because we seemed to be in a good place. I had just moved into my own apartment and I was helping him and his team start their non-profit organization. We just wrapped up a performance that we had been preparing for, for months and I was traveling for my pageant press tour. The day after the performance, I flew to Atlanta for my first stop on the tour and everything seemed normal. I never communicated my plan with him, and I was glad I didn't because a voluntary breakup no longer seemed necessary. I quickly learned that when God gives you instructions, it's better to obey immediately than to allow yourself time to rationalize against them.

If only I knew what was on the other side of my disobedience, I would have never neglected to follow the clear instructions God had given me. Less than 7 days later, God broke us up after a terrible argument. It's a situation I never shared because I always said our breakup was a "mutual" decision. But truth be told, we broke up after having an argument that led to him shoving me in my apartment. I never told anybody that detail because a part of me still believed we would get back together; in the event that we did reunite, I didn't want to be judged for staying in the relationship.

After that incident took place, I let a few days go by before reaching out to him. In the back of my mind, I wondered why he hadn't called me first. I thought that this was just going to be another one of our 24-hour breakups. I wanted him to be the one crawling back to me, begging for forgiveness, but he didn't. He didn't even call. A part of me felt desperate because I wanted him to initiate communication first, but I pushed my pride to the side and mustered up the courage to call.

It rang a few times. "Hello?" I said.

"Yeah…" He answered in a belittling, demeaning tone, "Why are you calling me? I don't want to be with you, don't ever call me again" as he hung up the phone.

I was crushed. I genuinely regretted ignoring God when I had the confidence to peacefully walk away. I felt incredibly rejected and hurt. The breakup seemed so easy for him, while I was swiftly falling into the worst depression of my life. If I could describe how I felt during this time, it was nothing short of a "hot, insecure mess." I found myself checking my phone constantly to see if I missed his call, purposely trying to bump into him at church, and trying to maintain relationships with his family and friends just so they can bring me up in conversations to him. I was desperate and I had allowed him to become my **god**. His presence, or lack thereof, completely controlled my emotions. The breakup was affecting every area of my life. My performance at work was slipping and I didn't know how to process the pain I was experiencing.

One morning a few weeks after our breakup, still completely and utterly depressed, I received a call from a recruiter in Dallas offering me a job if I was willing to relocate the next month. I was shocked because I had been wanting to move to Dallas; a few of my friends lived there, and every time I visited, it felt like home. Even though I desired to live there, I knew I wasn't going to voluntarily move without a job lined up. After 5 rounds of interviews and only nine diminutive months living in Houston, I accepted the position and prepared to move to Dallas. Although relocating was the best option for me, I know that a part of me would have dropped everything if my ex would have asked me to stay. Thank God he didn't.

One thing I learned is that God wants our trust. He is constantly raising red flags in our sight to warn us from heartbreak and destruction. When we blatantly avoid His guidance for our own selfish desires, it can take us down a path of destruction that could have easily been avoided. I know for a fact that if I would have taken advantage of the peaceful exit in November 2011, it would have saved me from the heart break and depression that resulted from my disobedience. God's warning gives us an opportunity to turn our focus back to him. And when we don't listen, sometimes He will destroy our plans before our plans destroy us.

CHAPTER 4

My Coldest Winter Ever

2011 was the year that changed my life. I have never experienced such crippling heartache and pain. I was a mess, totally heartbroken, and lonely. I was fresh out of a toxic relationship, settling in a new city for the second time that year, miles away from family, and working at a job that I soon began to hate. My living situation in Dallas was nowhere near glamorous, either. I slept on the floor of my sorority sister's apartment for months and "rock bottom" doesn't come close to the condition I would use to describe my life then. It was one of the hardest times in my life. It was my coldest winter ever. I would sleep on the floor bundled up in the corner with layered sweatshirts, sweat pants, gloves, and a blanket because the temperature would be so cold in the apartment. I didn't have the audacity to ask my sorority sister to adjust the temperature because I was barely paying her anything to live there. I didn't have a bed, a dresser, or anything. I had to make it with what I had.

I remember one night, I was reading a story in the Bible (Deuteronomy 1:2) about how it took the Israelites 40 years to take an 11-day trip to the promised land after many unnecessary conflicts. They spent forty years wandering around aimlessly instead of reaching their goal. This spoke to me in two ways. First: change is a journey. Second: if you don't learn from your mistakes, you can spend far more time wandering than God ever intended. At that moment, I made a decision to grow through my pain.

My ex and I had a few conversations after our break up and I knew it wasn't healthy to keep things lingering on. I hated how I was left in suspense about whether or not we would ever get back together again. It was becoming obvious to me that I needed to let go. I didn't want to be one of those women who spent years holding on to the thought of what could be. I wanted to be healed, whole, and happy again. I decided to go on a 40-day fast cutting off all communication with him because I knew I still had healing to do. Every time I heard his name I would feel some type of way and if someone

would ask, "What happened to you and him?"
I wanted to be able to answer without breaking
down.

Sometimes you find yourself in the middle
of nowhere, and sometimes in the middle of
nowhere, you find yourself. One night during
the fast, I was having an exceptionally hard day.
I got on Facebook and out of nowhere I kept
seeing statuses pop up about pursuing healthy
relationships, knowing your worth, how "God's
best is waiting for you." This was unusual,
being that my Facebook feed was typically
filled with worldly shenanigans. The person
who was posting theses statuses was a girl I
met in DC earlier that year who was sharing
someone's posts on her Facebook page with
the initials "HL." I thought to myself, "who
is this mysterious 'HL' person?" With a little

investigating, I found out that "HL" was a woman named Heather Lindsey. After scrolling through her page and being incredibly inspired, I decided to add her as a friend. At this time, Heather Lindsey didn't have a ministry. She was just a young woman on Facebook sharing quotes and scriptures empowering women to not settle in their relationships. She also shared her story about not kissing her husband until their wedding day. Her testimony sparked my curiosity to dive deeper into what she was teaching.

I read her blogs, went to her page for encouragement, and listened to her Tuesday night calls. I had no idea how much that virtual encounter would change the trajectory of my life and my relationships. I get teary-eyed even thinking about it, because it was the God in her and the example she set that made me want my own personal relationship with Christ. It was the first time in my entire life that I saw someone I could relate to who loved Jesus. She transparently shared her journey about giving her life to Christ and it inspired me to take a good look at the decisions I was making.

CHAPTER 5

I Almost Married the Wrong Guy

After almost a year after that breakup, I felt restored, healthy, and excited for what the future held. I dated every now-and-then, but relationships weren't my main focus until the unexpected happened. A college boyfriend made his way back into my life after a seven-year hiatus. When I was 17 years old, my freshman year in college, I met a guy who I thought was my "first love." I fell in what I thought was "love," but shortly after he transferred to play football at another school, we broke up.

For years I believed that we would reunite. I purposely kept a spot in my heart for him. Even though I was dating and had a few relationships, my soul was clearly still tied to his. A soul tie is an emotional bond or connection that unites you with someone else. They can be formed from relationships, physical, or emotional intimacy. For example, when you are intimate with someone, you become one flesh with that person. Your spirit, emotions, and every aspect of your being is united with that person. It is not just a physical act, but you become spiritually connected as well. One of the meanings of the word "joined" in the Greek means "glued to;" so when you have sex with someone that you are not married to, you become glued to them. Whenever you pull apart something that has been glued together, there is always damage to one or both parts. It is often very painful to disconnect the parts. That is why there tends to be emotional trauma after an intimate relationship ends.

I didn't know this as a young adult. It seemed like no matter what I did to get rid of feelings of him, he would pop back up in my life. He never showed any real interest, but nevertheless I would think, "Oh, he called to wish me happy birthday! Maybe there is still something there."

As I grew in my walk with Christ, he was no longer in the forefront of my mind, but I would be lying if I said I didn't do social media check-ins or respond to some of his messages from time-to-time. After seven years of off-and-on communication, he came back into my life *for real* this time. One night when I was praying about my future husband, the

Holy Spirit put him on my heart while I was journaling. I thought to myself, "okay, maybe he *is* my husband." I had a dream about him that same night, and he randomly called me the next day. Once again, I thought this was a sign. I hadn't spoken to him in a couple of years and at this point, he was playing football in the NFL, studying to be a pastor, and looking for a wife! Instantly, I assumed it was me. I called my mom and best friends, and prayed about our relationship. Shortly after this happened, we met in Atlanta. We discussed a lot of things from marriage, to purpose, to me possibly relocating to Atlanta. He took me on a tour of his new home while asking for my interior design input. I was so excited and thought, "this is for real this time!" Throughout the years, he would string me a long, not ever being clear on what his intentions were, and this was the first time he was actually making effort to talk about us getting back together. After a few conversations, I couldn't resist myself. I told him that God showed me he was my husband while I was journaling one night. YIKES! (Disclaimer, I don't ever recommend anyone revealing that to a man, if it was really God speaking, he will reveal it to both parties in due time). He was a little caught off guard, but my comment didn't totally scare him away.

It appeared as if things were lining up. But the main thing that was not lining up was the fact that *he did not pursue me and the peace of God was not in it*. I initiated everything in that relationship. He didn't make any effort to get to know the "adult" me, and everything felt forced. Before the football season started, I flew to visit him during training camp. I will never forget how irritated I was when he asked me to buy my own plane ticket. He said that he would reimburse me when I got there, but it still rubbed me the wrong way. I reluctantly agreed, and when it was time for me to leave and I told him to stop at the ATM for my "reimbursement," he acted as if it was an inconvenience to him. His trepidation to reimburse me for the flight was a red flag, along with the fact that he would go MIA for weeks. I would think, "I'm about to go *ring shopping* with a man like this?" I fell in love with the idea of being married to an NFL player—not him. So, after months of confusion, I prayed and asked God to show me what was going on. I had no idea what to do and I needed clarity.

One evening, the Holy Spirit directed me to call a close friend of mine. I told her everything I was going through from the glamorous parts to the parts I was ashamed to admit. She prayed with me and at the end of the phone call she said, "Ashley, God is saying, lay it down. He said that you have stepped out of your role as a woman and it is time to move on." This is why it's so crucial to have friends who can intercede for you. I knew from scripture that a "Man who finds a wife, finds a good thing and obtains favor from the Lord," (Proverbs 8:22) I was at peace knowing that my role was not to be the finder or convincer. I was relieved because deep down I knew God was confirming what I already felt in my spirit. But more importantly, I knew that soul tie had to be broken. I prayed and verbally asked God to break that tie on both ends, and it was a supernatural experience where I immediately felt the weight lifted off of me. I was finally able to let go and accept the fact that he was not my husband and we would never be together again.

Sometimes, God will bring people or relationships into our lives that do not last or aren't quite right for the sole purpose of allowing you to reference those negative experiences in the future to be grateful for what he has in store. There were many times I questioned why God didn't allow a relationship to work out when there were so many "signs" that it was meant to be. Truth is that oftentimes, when you think you are missing out on something good, you are being redirected to something great—something that's so much better than your past, that you'll look back and praise God for allowing certain situations to end.

I wanted to share this story, because I am so grateful that God showed me why certain relationships didn't work out so better ones could fall into place. I'm grateful for all the doors he forced shut because He knew I would never voluntarily close them. I'm grateful that he allowed my exes to be examples of the type of man He didn't want in my life. I am so incredibly grateful. I know a lot of people have past relationships that they can't quite let go of; I want you to know that you must be *emotionally* ready for who God has for you, and that starts by laying all of your baggage and past hurts at His feet. God introduced me to my husband shortly after I let go of the relationship with the NFL player because I was emotionally ready for him. I was finally free from my past relationships; he was the final door that needed to be closed.

Prior to meeting my husband, I asked God to reveal anyone that my soul was tied to. After writing down the names, I asked him to break those ties and I **believed** by faith they were broken. Breaking soul ties is a major key to having a successful relationship in the future. I remember listening to a broadcast on "Focus on the Family," a Christian ministry and radio broadcast, where couples who had been married for decades called in to share marriage advice on what kept them together for so long. It was inspiring to hear the marvelous bits of wisdom from all the couples, but one caller called in sharing a different perspective. She stated that she had been married for 17 years, and her husband left her for his high school sweet heart. Her advice to the listeners was to fervently pray that all soul ties are broken when you get into a new relationship, so they would not have to experience what she went through. Her message resonated with me and I pray that you heed to her advice.

CHAPTER 6
"Single, Saved & Secure"

As I started making my relationship with God a priority, I noticed that He was indeed preparing me for my purpose and marriage. I started to proactively approach my spiritual life and self-development. I used my time to figure out what I wanted to do and what made me tick. Spending time with God and studying His word ultimately prepared me to be in a relationship that glorified Him. I took my eyes off of marriage and focused on Christ and getting my life together spiritually, mentally, and physically. I didn't want to go into my next relationship with emotional baggage and insecurity. I started to explore my curiosities and live my life to the fullest. I went on mission trips, joined a life group at my church, traveled the world, started my own business, went to graduate school, and developed friendships with women who were like-minded. I managed my finances and paid off many of my debts and took care of myself physically. The issue with a lot of people who are desiring to be in a relationship is that they have high expectations for their future spouse but they don't put any effort in their own personal development. Then, they wonder why they keep attracting the same type of guy.

Although I was single, I wasn't desperate. During this time, I was continually being pursued by good, Christian men; professional athletes, lawyers, surgeons, and more. I have stories for days about my experiences, but I learned that just because a guy pursues you, doesn't mean you have to entertain his advances. Deep down I knew these men weren't who God meant for me to be with, so I stopped wasting my time and theirs. A man's status, money or fame did not alter my level of attraction to him. I knew too many people who were married to outwardly "successful" men, yet were miserable. A lot of women continue to say "yes" to any and every man that approaches them because they do not have the confidence or faith to say "no." They don't believe that God is in control and that He will align them with who they need to be with. When you are desperate and impatient, you are more likely to go on dates with anyone who asks you out because you fear missing out on the "one." I was able to politely turn people down because I trusted God. As my level of confidence increased, I no longer felt pressured to date or go out just to "meet someone" or "be seen." I was able to walk away from situations that didn't feel right in my spirit, even when I didn't have a "justifiable" reason not to date someone. I was able to discern which men to turn down because the Holy Spirit would clearly place red flags and stop signs in my view. When someone shows you who they are, believe them. I didn't waste time pretending I didn't see certain qualities just to be in a relationship. I had standards, and I wasn't willing to settle.

I believed that my husband was somewhere preparing for me, so I would pray for him. I would pray that he was aligned with where God wanted him to be and that God would bring us together when it was the best time for the both of us. There was something in me that was excited about when, how, and where I would meet my husband, but I didn't fixate on it. I lived my life, expected the best, and I didn't beg God for something that I knew would eventually happen. I became laser-focused on allowing God to renew my mind and my heart. I cut off all distractions by changing my number to avoid random guys from my past reaching out to me. I didn't want anyone from my past to catch me in a moment of boredom or weakness.

I guarded my heart from conversations where the topic constantly surrounded marriage, infidelity, or anything that spoke against the blessing of marriage. Many times, when you are single, you have friends who are single who always want to talk about relationships, attend singles conferences, read books on being single, join groups on being single, and are just obsessed with being single! That wasn't me. I intentionally avoided making relationships an idol and doing so helped me to not over-analyze my situation.

CHAPTER 7

Why Some Christian Men got the Side Eye...

There was a time in my life when I thought dating a saved man was unappealing. Of course, my desire was to be equally-yoked, and be with someone who had a serious relationship with the Lord, but I was turned-off by many of the men I would encounter. I was approached by all kinds of Christian men but I would be completely put-off by the corny jokes and constant interjecting of scriptures in ordinary conversations. One guy in particular told me that, "God told him I was the one," and I about choked on my drink. We knew each other for 2 days. I was disgusted.

Not to mention, I was still very unfamiliar with the concept of "courting," and although I was praying for a husband with charm and faith, I couldn't help but hope God would bless me with a man that had swagger, and one that I wouldn't mind being, um... "fruitful" with. I wanted my spouse to be attractive and also relatable. Someone that I could laugh and joke with and discuss deeper spiritual things. I wanted someone who could not only be the leader of our household, but also lead the cupid shuffle, or the wobble, lol.

In a way, I was projecting my true feelings about myself onto my future relationship. I had a fear that I was becoming more spiritually mature than any guys my age and I that I wouldn't be able to relate to any of them. I was studying the word and going to Bible studies and conferences, but I noticed that men at church tended to be the minority. I had to surrender this fear to God and change my belief in order to not lose hope. Instead of thinking the man I desired was a rare find, I chose to believe that, just how I was preparing and developing as an individual, my husband was somewhere doing the same.

CHAPTER 8

My List vs. God's Best

When I first met, or should I say when I first saw my husband's profile on Instagram, I didn't immediately think he was the "one." I thought he was attractive, but he was the polar opposite of what I was used to dating. I was used to dating men who were very tall with a dark complexion. My tallest boyfriend was 6'10"! Since I'm a frequent wearer of high heels and I'm 5'8", I always preferred dating men who were taller than me with heels on. I had a "list" of all the qualities and characteristics I desired in a spouse and paid no attention to prospects that didn't match up. One late evening, I was strolling around Wal-Mart and I stumbled upon the book and magazine aisle. I'm an avid reader and I can get lost skimming and scanning through books and magazines. It is one of my favorite hobbies. I picked up an unfamiliar magazine that had many great positive and self-development articles in it. I read an article by a woman by the name of Kathleen Kastner who discussed the correlation of finding a mate as it relates to how you view yourself. The article was so enlightening that I bought the magazine, went home, and looked her up online to see if she had any other empowering content. I saw she authored a book, so I immediately ordered it to learn more about her perspective on dating and relationships. It took me less than a week to finish her book. The biggest lesson I learned was the importance of surrendering your list for God's best. I decided to give up my superficial pattern of dating and completely trashed my list. The day I finished the book, I tore up my list into little pieces and threw it out my car window (sorry mother nature) and I asked God to send the man that was in His will for me. Not even three weeks after that day, I met Carrington. The first thing I asked him was, "How tall are you?"

I believe a lot of people are still single because they are sticking to their guns concerning what they desire in a mate and won't relinquish control to God. If you have a laundry-list that gets longer year after year… live a little. It's important to have standards and deal-break-ers, but understand that people are constantly growing and developing. Keep an open mind to God's will, not your personal agenda. If your list hasn't served you thus far, trash it! Be open to the relationship God has for you, even if it doesn't match the image you created in your mind. When you are open to God's will, it removes the blinders from your eyes, and opens up a world of possibilities. Be flexible and discerning. God sends you what you need—not always what you want.

CHAPTER 9
Child, Please

"It was an improbable romance. He was a country boy. She was from the city. She had the world at her feet, while he didn't have two dimes to rub together." -The Notebook

Carrington and I met before we ever laid eyes on each other. I expected to meet someone like him—someone who would love me like Christ loves the church; someone who was in agreement that a thriving, successful marriage was possible. I believe my expectation and trust in God was the magnet that brought us together. Matthew18:19 says, "Again, truly I tell you that if two of you on earth agree about anything they ask for, it will be done for them by my Father in heaven." This is a powerful revelation because, although Carrington and I didn't meet until an appointed time, we were in spiritual agreement prior to us meeting in person.

When Carrington first reached out to me on social media, I almost overlooked him completely. It was the day after I finished a 24-hour fast that included me cutting off all social media and my cell phone. I literally sat in my apartment on July 4th (American Independence Day) and spent time with God, while everyone else was celebrating and attending barbeques. I felt myself going through a spiritual transition, and I knew going on a fast was what I needed to do instead of going out with friends. The next day when I turned on my phone, Carrington had "liked" and commented on several of my pictures, and I was curious to see who he was. I went to his page and noticed that he was a football player at the college I graduated from, and that he was 3 years younger than me. I immediately thought, "child, *please*." What could he possibly have to offer? He was still in college, working at a part-time job, saving up for a car, and living with his mom. I was swiftly about to put him in the friend-zone. Here I was in my first year of graduate school, with a good job, a new car, and billion-dollar dreams; I never imagined myself dating someone *younger* than me. I judged him before I ever had a real conversation with him. But something told me to give him a chance, to try something different, and to keep an *open* heart...

Keeping an open heart was one of the best decisions I ever made. If I would have judged Carrington for the season he was in when I first met him, I could have easily missed out on the most amazing love story God was writing on my behalf. Our relationship is a prime example of what it looks like to build an empire together, starting from the bottom. There was a time when we weren't even able to order dessert at a restaurant, but we now have the ability to eat the best foods, and give to others. We have learned the importance of being a great steward of what God has blessed us with and taking advantage of higher education. Many people may read this and think it must have been tough dating someone who didn't "have it all together" but truthfully, it wasn't. It was actually a lot of fun because we learned how to make it work with what we had and we both knew God had a plan.

I'm thankful I met Carrington in that season because I was able to witness firsthand how God transformed my boyfriend into a husband, and eventually the provider of our family, allowing me to become the "housewife" and mom-trepreneur that I've always desired to be.

I wanted to share this so that people know that although the present circumstances of someone's life may not be glamorous, it doesn't mean that God doesn't have a plan. It saddens me to see women pass up great men over temporary material things. Many women want a man that is already established, but I have learned that an obedient woman will not only be a part of the expansion process, but she will also be his biggest cheerleader along the way. Eliminating a man just because he doesn't have all the material things you want at that very moment could lead to a life of regret. If a man has vision and produces the fruit of taking action, stick by his side. Empires are built together. Sometimes loving someone along their path to success not only shows your trust in the Lord, but it also unveils the true condition of your heart.

CHAPTER 10
Guilt, Shame, and Forgiveness

Prior to getting into a relationship with Carrington, I was not a virgin, but I was abstinent. I was abstinent for two reasons: **First**, I was determined to be sexually pure until marriage; **second**, I believed that my next boyfriend would be my husband. I will be honest, I got one out of the two right. My boyfriend *did* become my husband, but we fell short in the area of abstinence. The major reason being was that we failed to set boundaries. Truthfully, we did not have the conversation on where we stood when it came to purity until after our first "mess up." We both knew that we didn't want our relationship to end up like the ones we had been in the past, where sex was the foundation and heartbreak was the outcome. I was so disappointed in myself and in Carrington that I was on the verge of ending our relationship. I told him that my relationship with God was more important than my relationship with him and if we couldn't wait until marriage, then we couldn't be together. He was in agreement, but I was so heavily convicted that I started to have doubts on whether that conversation was enough to keep us on track. I was struggling to forgive myself for "knowing better," and I couldn't shake the disappointment I was facing. We decided to make a change and be proactive rather than reactive. On a Saturday evening in November 2013, we met with a pastor at church who was willing to pray with us and provide truthful tips on how to move forward guilt-free. We prayed, cried, and repented. At that meeting, Carrington essentially told me that he wanted to marry me and be obedient to what God was calling us to do. That night, we officially transitioned from "dating" to "dating with purpose."

Carrington had a little bit more insight than me on dating with purpose or what some call "courting," but our combined knowledge was meager. I still thought courting was a bunch of rules we had to follow before saying "I do." I would watch videos and read blogs on other couples' courting experiences, but instead of feeling inspired, I would beat myself up and compare everything they were doing right to everything we had done wrong. I had to release feelings of inadequacy and embrace the fact that every setback is an opportunity for a comeback and that there was still hope for our story.

In the beginning, we tried a lot of different things, like no longer staying the night at each other's houses, and leaving before a certain time, but it almost seemed like the temptation was getting worse. Marriage was the topic of many discussions and although getting engaged appeared to be in the distant future, we needed to make changes *now* in order to avoid sinning. What we identified is that when there were no boundaries in place, we were completely led by our emotions, which left an open door for the devil. Purity is not something that can be accomplished through legalistic rules; you must have a heart that desires to please God. This desire will trump the need to fulfill your lustful desires. It took us a while to see that we had to completely depend on God in this area, but we made a choice and commitment to practice abstinence until marriage. Our commitment included stopping anything that tempted us— including kissing. We decided to put our energy toward building a spiritual foundation that would allow for the healthiest marriage possible. We didn't want to jeopardize our relationship or the calling that God had on our lives.

It was challenging, yet incredibly rewarding. We had our ups and our downs, but we kept the course. Repentance saved our lives. Some people think God won't be able to use them because of their sin, but that is so far from the truth. God uses imperfect people so that unbelievers can relate to them. Nobody is perfect and it is refreshing to see how God will use someone's "mess" to become their "message." This is beneficial to unbelievers because it gives them the opportunity to relate to someone who has rededicated their life to Christ.

Purity doesn't mean that we are better than anyone else, it means that we are called to encourage and edify one another to live in a way that honors God. Anyone can turn from their sin right now, repent, and start fresh. If you are in a situation that you know displeases the Lord, I recommend that you stop reading right now and lift up a prayer to Him. Ask God to forgive you for your sin, the ones you have committed knowingly and unknowingly. Ask Him to renew your heart and your mind and give you the strength to live in purity. The Bible says old things pass away and we are made new in Christ Jesus (2 Cor. 5:17). When you give Him your past, don't pick it back up and don't let the raggedy devil try to mess with your mind about who you used to be.

CHAPTER 11

Pre-Engagement Counseling— Weird or Wise?

After Carrington and I had our initial session with the pastor that evening, we ended up going back for another. I still do not remember how a counseling session transitioned into full-blown "pre-engagement/marital" counseling, but it did. Looking back, I can't help but think about how God works everything out, even when we feel like we least deserve it. If Carrington and I would not have sought *help* in the areas we struggled, I know for a fact that we would not have voluntarily started going to counseling. Although we spoke about getting married, the truth of the matter was, we both were finishing up school and assumed marriage was something we would pursue years down the line. At least that was *my* assumption.

On March 28th, 2014, 8 months and 5 counseling sessions later, I hosted an event called "The Forgotten First Love" in Dallas, Texas where over 400 women gathered together to fellowship to hear from phenomenal speakers, one of them being Heather Lindsey. To this day, I am still amazed by how God brought everything full-circle. Never did I imagine that I would be hosting an event and sharing a stage with a woman who I had been so inspired by from afar. It was an amazing experience, but little did I know there was a surprise at the end that would change the course of my life forever.

Towards the end of the event, I was so excited to leave so I could call Carrington to tell him how amazing the event went, but there were a few more items left on the agenda. When it was time to end the conference, I introduced the founder of the organization to give her closing remarks. As I handed her the microphone, she gracefully asked her executive team to come to the stage. As she expressed her appreciation and gratitude for all their hard work, she then directed her attention to me and said, "Ashley, we appreciate you hosting this event. As a token of our appreciation, we have a surprise for you. Will you please close your eyes?" My immediate thought was, "Close my eyes... for *what*?" I saw some flowers in her hand, so I automatically thought, "maybe those were for me? ... but why do I need to close my eyes to get some flowers?"

I hesitantly closed my eyes, and then a member of the executive team proceeded to cover my eyes with her hands to ensure there was no peeking.

"Can we please have Ashley's surprise come to the stage?" I heard someone announce.

For the next 5 seconds, I heard roaring and screaming, and as the executive member slid her hand away from my eyes, I opened them to see Carrington down on one knee.

"Will you marry me, Ashley?"

I looked around in utter shock as the tears welled up in my eyes. *Was I dreaming? Is this for real?!*

The executive team member nudged me and

said, "He asked you to marry him, girl!" I still couldn't believe what was going on.

"YES! YES! I will marry you!"

Carrington had been back stage for almost two hours waiting for the green light to come out for this big moment. I was so shocked that he took initiative to reach out to the organization to request permission to propose. I was elated, and the ring was absolutely stunning. Engraved inside of the band was eight hearts that symbolized the eight months we dated prior to getting engaged. Even more charming—it was my mother's birthday! Both her and Carrington's mom were in the audience witnessing our special moment!

CHAPTER 12

How I Knew He was the "One"

Prior to getting engaged, many people asked me how I knew Carrington was the "one." Of course, every relationship is different, so I will simply share my personal experience. I explain it like a puzzle. When you are putting a puzzle together, you see many pieces that look like they could possibly match, and some actually *almost* fit; however, you know that if you force it, it will throw off the entire puzzle. So, you toss the mismatched pieces back in the bunch until you find the piece with the right fit. When you get it, you immediately know because the fit is seamless.

In my experience, finding the "one" was a simple connection that felt natural, unforced, and intentional. This was my experience with Carrington. It was not a dramatic moment with flashing lights and an orchestra swelling in crescendo behind us; it was a simple peace that cannot be easily articulated. When you stop trying to force the wrong pieces to fit, the puzzle will eventually come together perfectly. It will be apparent, and you will confidently move on to another section of your masterpiece knowing that you made the right choice.

CHAPTER 13
Twelve Days of Purity

While Carrington and I were engaged, we did many things to prepare for marriage. This included everything from prayer, to fasting, to mapping out our dreams and goals, to financial planning, learning each other's love languages, and so much more. We were intentional about getting to know one another on a deeper level and we were committed to being open and honest. One thing we didn't discuss was past relationships. We didn't believe it was necessary to intentionally rehash the details of prior relationships because they were irrelevant. I believe it's important to not share extensive details about the specifics of your past relationships. This helps to avoid feelings of comparison and jealousy. You want to make sure that you are protecting your spouse and yourself from insecurity.

In our relationship, we have had past relationships resurface due to work-related events, but communication was never intentionally initiated with those exes. I modeled on a TV show with one of Carrington's exes, and the Holy Spirit told me who she was prior to my attendance to the event. I remember looking over the final instructions for the shoot and I noticed that the coordinator included all the other women who were a part of the event on the same email. When I saw her name, something in my spirit indicated that was Carrington's ex-girlfriend. It was clear as day. I called Carrington, and told him what the Holy Spirit revealed to me. I was right. I appreciate God giving me the heads-up, because I was able to mentally prepare. I didn't find it necessary to be overly friendly, but I was kind and sweet. There was no awkwardness, and we both nailed the show.

Leading up to our wedding, one of the most significant things we did was fast from each other for an entire 12 days before our wedding. Our decision to fast was not a mere attempt to be religious; it was 100% necessary. We were starting to fall back into temptation. It felt like as the days got closer to saying, "I do," the devil was attacking us more than ever. To prevent us from compromising our purity, we decided to commit to fasting from one another. The fast meant: no talking on the phone, no hanging out, no texting, and no communication whatsoever. At times, I wanted to give up because with our wedding a couple of weeks away, there were still so many things to be discussed. It was a major test of our faith.

It was one of the hardest times of my life. To this day, the only way I can describe it is 12 days of spiritual warfare. Nothing went wrong in particular, but I felt uneasy in my spirit. Although 12 days does not seem like a long time, I was incredibly emotional because deep down, I missed Carrington. It was the longest we ever went without talking or seeing one another, but I knew I had to be productive instead of moping around wishing the days would speed by.

While we were on the fast, I remember being at home alone on Day Four when God spoke to me. He brought my attention to my prayer box that I had been keeping for the past two years. My prayer box was used to surrender my desires, prayers, and frustrations to God. I would take a small piece of paper, write my prayer, say my prayer, and thank God that it was already done before putting it in the box. My goal was to avoid worrying about things that were out of my control and to keep track of the things that I was grateful for. That night, I sat on my bedroom floor sorting out all the prayers that God answered versus the ones that were still pending. The pile of answered prayers was enormous in comparison to the pile of the few unanswered and ongoing prayers. I sat there in complete gratitude knowing that some of the prayers that seemed so imperative at the time, were "no's" or "not now's" in God's plan.

As I sorted through the pile, I came across a specific prayer that read, *"My perfect husband, please let me be ready for him and him ready for me—August 21st, 2012."* I wrote that prayer asking God to prepare me for marriage, while I was single with no prospects in sight. All I had was faith and confidence that giving my relationship status over to God was the wisest thing I could do. Almost two years later from the date of that prayer, I was less than a week away from marrying my best friend.

I cannot tell you how many times I prayed for the wrong situations to result in marriage. My life would be so different if I had not surrendered my relationship status over to God. When I finally made the decision to trust God with my entire life,

He took everything I had and upgraded it. I love the wisdom in the story of Cinderella when the fairy godmother transformed Cinderella's existing circumstances into something miraculous by simply using what she already had. She transformed her rags into a ball gown, her pumpkin into a coach, and her mice into horseman. I'm not saying that God is our fairy godmother or some kind of genie; what I am saying is that when we choose to stop settling for what we think is best, the Holy Spirit is able to work freely in our lives.

Day Four of the fast eventually turned into Day 12. When Carrington and I reunited, I was not surprised that he grew spiritually as well. He shared with me the impact the 12 days had on him and how grateful he was that we sacrificed communication in order to protect the purity of our relationship. In less than 24 hours, we would be walking down the aisle! It all felt so surreal.

CHAPTER 14

Jumping the Broom

I had imagined my wedding day since I was a little girl. I knew that I wanted something memorable and exquisite. Little did I know that "exquisite" weddings were far from cheap. Although we were excited for the wedding planning process, we were naïve when it came to the cost of carrying out a dream wedding. We went from contemplating eloping, to a surprise wedding, to getting married in a courthouse, to a destination wedding, and then finally God said, "wait on Me."

We prayed, believed, and put our faith into action. God took our *little* plans and transformed them into something beautiful. He provided for us beyond what we asked for or even imagined. Still to this day, our wedding day felt like a dream. We planned our wedding in four-and-a-half months and I still don't know how we managed to pull that off predominately stress-free.

Our wedding day was impeccable. At 1:00 pm, I arrived at our wedding venue after a morning of prayer, massages, and quiet-time. Waking up that day was 1,000 times more exciting than Christmas morning. For weeks, we prayed for great weather, being that we planned an outdoor ceremony in Texas on a day that could have potentially been one of the hottest days of the summer. Thankfully, God answered yet another prayer, allowing our special day to be in the high 70's rather than the predicted 100's.

As I walked down the aisle, in my sweetheart neckline, ornate wedding gown that framed my silhouette beautifully, I can remember every single emotion, tear, and smile. It was sheer euphoria that protected my makeup from becoming tarnished by streams of tears. It was so touching to see all the friends and family who traveled from all across the world to share that special moment with us. Every single thing worked out—from the beautiful weather on our wedding day to me not being on my menstrual cycle for the honeymoon. I know I could have spared that detail, but let's be real—that was an answered prayer, too.

Years later, I am still in awe of how everything

unfolded. God continues to outdo himself in our marriage. We are in divine alignment. We asked God to give us our wedding date, and not only did He give us the date, but He also gave us the venue, the wedding planner, and a beautiful honeymoon. I share this to simply show the outcome of walking by faith and obedience. We are no better than anyone, and from what I shared about our past, we are far from perfect. The faithfulness of God is what led us to where we are today. He hears every prayer and meets every need. Don't be so laser-focused on *your* plans that you completely miss out on what He is trying to do in your life. Don't be afraid to dream, to ask, and to thank Him, even when things don't go your way. Relinquishing control and walking by faith can be scary, but it is such a fulfilling experience when you are able to witness God's faithfulness firsthand.

CHAPTER 15

Why Marriage isn't "Hard" for Everyone

Prior to getting married, one thing I constantly heard was that "marriage is hard." People didn't necessarily elaborate on what they meant by that, they would just throw the statement around like a generic cliché. When I would hear this, it made me feel uneasy and gave me a sense of trepidation. Perhaps they meant, living together is hard? Being selfless is hard? But how can marriage in general be dismissively classified as "hard" when each one is so different? Whether it's true for some couples or not, I wish it wasn't embedded into the minds of people who haven't had the chance to experience it for themselves.

When you get to the point in life where you understand the meaning and purpose of marriage, it extinguishes the pessimistic claims. Knowing the purpose of marriage allows you the freedom to move forward to write your own story. My desire is that I would not reinforce the saying that marriage is "hard," because it's the best thing that has ever happened to me. Just like anything in life, relationships can present character-building opportunities, but "hard" is not the word I would use to describe it. Marriage is not an act of toiling in the fields; it's building a life with a person you love and cherish. It's a ministry, and it doesn't look the same for everyone.

It turns out, the people who have great relationships make a lot of purposeful *choices* on how to interact with one another. Couples who have "figured out" the key to maintaining a healthy, thriving relationship simply implement positive habits that become second-nature to them, thus creating a rhythm that results in a pleasant marriage. It's like gaining weight—either you will control it over time, or let it go until you are 60lbs overweight, wondering when the change occurred. You will either gradually destroy your relationship or make small daily deposits to contribute to the success of it.

Bottom-line: healthy relationships don't just happen, they are a result of intentional activity. Whether you are single, dating, or married, it's important to remember that having a strong spiritual foundation is the first step to any healthy relationship. Although storms, winds, and rain may come, you can look out the window *knowing* that your house will continue to stand firm. You have that security in Christ. You can have complete and total trust that, once the storm passes, your house will still stand intact.

CHAPTER 16

When Hot Mess Meets Housewife

Throughout my journey, one of my biggest goals was to become a "housewife" and a stay-at-home "mom-trepreneur." By definition, a "mom-treprenuer" is a woman who nurtures her entrepreneurial endeavors while simultaneously juggling her home and family life. I love how the Proverbs 31 woman was not only a wife of noble character, but also a business woman. I have always been a very ambitious person, and I knew deep down that God had given me vision and purpose through being a wife, mother, and an entrepreneur. Over the years, I have observed how many women "lose" themselves in motherhood, and although my desire is to be the CEO of our home; I believe that you do not have to sacrifice who you are called to be in order to be effective in your home.

One of the most rewarding things you can do is honor who you are in each season of your life. I have spent many years of my life building other people's dreams, and now I'm grateful that I am able to build my own. I have innately known that a major part of my calling revolves around relationships and empowering people to live their best life. I would never be able to do what I do now without my husband. There would be no "Ashley Empowers" without him. There would be no relationship empowerment without him. He is my answered prayer. I am now able to raise my daughter while also fully walking in my calling as a housewife and entrepreneur. I wake up every morning extremely blessed to be in alignment with my assignment. I have gone through seasons of loneliness, testing, pruning, and silence, which all gave my faith a chance to grow.

If I can give you one piece of advice, I want to encourage you to design a life that you are proud of. Ask yourself, "what do I truly want?" What do you believe God is calling you to do? Don't be influenced by what other people are doing in their life. Set your own sail! Live a life that is full of purpose and faith, from your relationships to your overall well-being. Dream the highest dream possible, because you become what you believe.

CHAPTER 17

The Best Relationship You Will Ever Have

In this book, we have discussed many different relationships, from failed relationships to "almost" relationships, and the relationship between my husband and I. But I cannot conclude this book without magnifying the best relationship you will ever have, and that is your personal relationship with God. Marriage is a minor theme in the Bible. The major theme is God. On your quest to be in a healthy relationship, don't forget that marriage is until death, but your relationship God is everlasting. Having a relationship with God will completely transform your life, and I believe that having a strong relationship with Him is a prerequisite to having a thriving relationship with another human being. Only God knows the future of your relationships, but no matter what situation you find yourself in, you can relax and know that you are exactly where you are meant to be.

It's easy to get distracted seeing endless posts on social media about engagements, beautiful weddings, honeymoons, and companionship, but you have to guard your heart. I have definitely experienced my share of social-media-hangovers, but at the end of the day, it's okay to have healthy desires of being in a relationship. Matthew 6:33 reminds us to "seek first his kingdom and his righteousness, and all these things will be given to you as well." This was my go-to scripture when I needed to center myself and remind myself that I never needed to seek a relationship; all I needed to do was focus on Jesus because He would provide for me.

You have to be very honest with yourself if you feel incomplete without being in a relationship. If this is you, the missing factor is most likely your relationship with God. When you get plugged into Him by praying every day, reading the Bible, surrounding yourself with a positive community, and being obedient, He will give you peace, wisdom and insight on areas where you need to grow and develop.

As I sit here writing the conclusion of this book as a full-time "housewife" and mom-trepreneur,

I can see my daughter peacefully swinging in her swing and I can't help but thank God for bringing everything full-circle. I longed to live in a household where both parents were present, healthy, and loving. I'm appreciative to say that I became the change I wanted to see. I broke the generational trend in my family to ensure that the generations after us will have a legacy of love and purpose.

I don't know where you are in your life, but I want you to know you have power. You do not have to settle in any area of your life. The decisions you make will have a rippling effect on the generations to come. Be selective. Choose wisely. When the Holy Spirit is leading your life and relationships, you will never take a loss. You don't have to be super religious to have a relationship with God either—just take baby steps. Include Him a little bit more in your everyday life and begin to seek his face rather than his hand. You will see a monumental shift in your desires and life. When this happens, I will not be surprised if you end up married.

CHAPTER 18

Bonus Chapter – 60 Bucket List Items for Singles

A Singles Girl's Journey to A Life of NO Regrets

"Man cannot discover new oceans unless he has the courage to lose sight of the shore."

–Andre Gide

When I was single, I took advantage of exploring my curiosities. I traveled, lived in different cities, went on mission trips, started businesses, and created beautiful memories. Now that I am married, I can yell from rooftops about how important it is to take advantage of your single season. Marriage is awesome, but it comes with many responsibilities. You simply don't have the same freedom you do as a single when you are married with kids. Take this time to enjoy your flexible schedule, explore your curiosities, and live the life of your wildest dreams! I prepared a bucket list of items that I would recommend every single person to do before marriage.

I have included some blank space for you to add any additional items that spark your interest. I recommend creating your own bucket list based on your age. For example, if you are 25 years old, add 25 things to your list.

1. Create a Prayer Box

2. Go on a mission trip

3. Make a domestic/international travel wish list

4. Take a vacation alone

5. Stay home all day and binge-watch Netflix and eat as much as you want

6. Watch the best-rated movie from the year you were born

7. Take yourself on a date

8. Treat yourself to the ultimate spa day. Get a mani, pedi, and even indulge in a massage.

9. Get a library card

10. Check out cookbooks and tryout different recipes

11. Live on your own (pay bills, clean up, grocery shop for yourself)

12. Go out for karaoke night

13. Travel for the weekend to see an old friend or family member

14. Go to a free sewing, scrapbooking, or crafting class

15. Take a cooking class

16. Attend a Bible study or small group meeting with some people from your church

17. Spend the afternoon at a homeless shelter feeding and sharing stories with those in need

18. Go on a hike somewhere you haven't been

19. Call in sick to work one day and spend the afternoon window-shopping downtown and trying a new restaurant

20. Spend a random night in the city and get a hotel. Order room service in a robe like a boss.

21. Live in another city

22. Teach abroad

23. Plan a weekend trip with your friends

24. Volunteer in your community helping children, saving the planet, rescuing animals, beautifying your city... tons of people need you.

25.   Lift weights

26.   Train for (and finish) a huge physical test like a half-marathon.

27.   Quit your job if you hate it. It feels so good to quit a job and not be affecting anyone else's livelihood.

28.   Learn to stand up for yourself

29.   Witness a once-in-a-lifetime thing

30.   Go on a date with someone who gives you butterflies.

31.   Buy yourself some flowers

32.   Buy something frivolous and expensive that you LOVE wearing

33.   Continue your education

34.   Babysit someone's baby

35.   Host a girls-only night

36.   Get in your best physical shape ever!

37.   Take last-minute, spontaneous trips

38.   Donate clothes you no longer wear

39. Go zip-lining

40. Try out a new hair style

41. Get a NEW hobby

42. Redecorate your room or your entire house

43. Go 24 hours without complaining

44. Set up a spiritual counseling session on your own

45. Go on a spiritual fast

46. Go speed-dating for the experience

47. Send Christmas cards

48. Do the very thing you are afraid to do

49. Go to your high school reunion

50. Audition for a commercial

51. Write a book

52. Do a photoshoot

53. Save $10,000+

54. Pay of your debt and get in the habit of tithing

55. Go on a safari

56. Take a business risk or switch careers

57. Read a lot of good books

58. Have a slumber party with your girlfriends

59. Go to a department store makeup section and get a free makeover

60. Plant a garden

61. Have a picnic and read a book at the park

62. Learn to paddleboard, bowl, or do some other sport you've been talking about.

63. Ask a man to help you carry something

64. Do a good deed. Walk someone's dog, watch someone's child while they do something fun, or shop for your elderly neighbor.

65. Start a gratitude journal

66. Get a pet

67. Learn to change a tire

68. Actively meet new people

69. Create a list of life goals

70. Take on a home improvement project for you or someone else

71. Accomplish a fitness goal

72. Learn a foreign language

73. Celebrate your birthday like a queen

74. Take a break from social media

75. Join an intramural sport

76. Establish a healthy prayer and reading life

77. Nurture the friendships you have in your life

78. Interview couples that have been married for 25+ years and find out what makes things work for them

79. Do a 3+ day juice detox

80. Read the 5 Love Languages for yourself. Find out YOUR love language and learn how to identify other love languages

81. Think 5, 10, 25, 50 years down the road what do you want your lifestyle to look like

82. Get in the habit of taking care of yourself mentally, spiritually, and physically now

Please note all these things can be done when you are married as well, these are a few suggestions to help you make the most out of this season!

My Personal Bucket List

1.

2.

3.

4.

5.

6.

7.

8.

9.

10.

11.

12.

13.

14.

15.

16.

17.

18.

19.

20.

21.

22.

23.

24.

25.

26.

27.

28.

29.

30.

31.

32.

33.

34.

35.

36.

37.

38.

39.

40.

41.

42.

43.

44.

45.

46.

47.

48.

49.

50.

51.

52.

53.

54.

55.

56.

57.

58.

59.

60.

61.

62.

63.

64.

65.

66.

67.

68.

69.

70.

71.

72.

73.

74.

75.

76.

77.

78.

79.

80.

81.

82.

83.

84.

85.

86.

87.

88.

89.

90.

91.

92.

93.

94.

95.

96.

97.

98.

99.

100.

Acknowledgements

God- Thank you for giving me the courage
to complete this assignment & thank you
Holy Spirit for speaking through me.

Thank you to everyone who supported and
encouraged me to share my journey.

About the Author

Ashley Brown, affectionately known as "Ashley Empowers," is a marriage advocate, relationship consultant, and a pioneer within the relationship community. She works daily to change the tone of the conversation about marriage and relationships around the world. She is the creator and host of "Dating with Purpose," a popular series and movement that promotes pursuing healthy relationships with God at the center. Ashley is happily married to Carrington Brown, her strongest advocate and partner in business and together they have a beautiful daughter.

Made in the USA
Columbia, SC
31 December 2017